CREATIVE WAYS TO LOVE & ENCOURAGE HER

DATING EDITION

JEFFERSON BETHKE

with RICH DE LA MORA

Published in Pasadena, CA, by Aloha and Rain. Aloha and Rain titles may be purchased in bulk for educational, business, fundraising, or sales promotional use. For information, please e-mail info@alohaandrain.com.

Unless otherwise noted, Scriptures are taken from the Holy Bible, New International Version®, NIV®. Copyright © 1973, 1978, 1984, 2011 by Biblica, Inc.™ Used by permission of Zondervan. All rights reserved worldwide. www.zondervan.com.

The Library of Congress Cataloging-in-Publication
Data is on file with the Library of Congress
ISBN-13: 978-0692091401

TABLE OF CONTENTS

DAY

HOW TO GET THE MOST OUT OF THIS BOOK

First off, you rock. By getting these paired books and wanting to go through them with your significant other, you obviously are already dominating at life! We have prayed over this project and believe it can be a fun way to cultivate a healthy relationship and bring back the joy and intimacy that sometimes gets lost amidst everyday activities.

To get the most out of this book, we'd first say lean in. Lean into the ideas, the spontaneity and the parts that stretch you the most. Don't be afraid to just go for it, have fun and create memories. We are firm believers that with these two books, whatever you put into it you will get out of it. Isn't that true with all our relationships as a whole? Also, know that this is just a template. Some things won't fit for your relationship, or you can't do based on certain locations, resources, and other variables. We have tried to make every day as applicable for everyone as possible. So with that being said, feel free to morph it, change it, adapt it and do whatever you need to do to get the most out of it. Because at the end of the day, the goal isn't to follow this book rigidly and *"cross each day off your checklist,"* but rather it's to bring a fresh vibrancy and life back to your relationship.

We are so excited to release this edition for couples who are dating and engaged! We teamed up with another married couple, Rich and Brittni De La Mora for their insight on dating. You will see comments from them throughout the book, we love and appreciate their wisdom and you will too! The next 31 days are going to bring fresh fire and excitement into your relationship. Have fun and keep us updated on social media by hashtagging #31CreativeWays.

JEFF & ALYSSA BETHKE

DAY ONE: PRAYER

Some of the most encouraging times ever in our marriage is when Alyssa tells me she's praying for me. Not just in general, but when she tells me what her prayer was. That she's praying for my walk with Jesus. That I'd come to know Him more deeply that day. She prays for my purity. That I'd protect and guard my thoughts.

Rich's Insight:

Prayer is a form of communication with God, but it's also how God communicates with us. When my wife expresses that she's praying for me, it drastically changes my day. Not only does it change my day, but I felt secure knowing that I have a partner on my side who's praying for me and is seeking God for me. There's an old saying that goes, *"The couple who prays together, stays together."* Prayer is the glue to your relationship that strengthens and unifies your relationship. Therefore we encourage you to pray.

Make a point to ask your girlfriend how she could use your prayers. Then sometime over the next week, write a prayer out for her on a card or piece of paper and give it to her. Or today, ask if you can pray for her aloud. When you do this, you will find peace, encouragement, and unity in your relationship.

JOURNAL BELOW:

WRITE WHAT YOU LEARNED TODAY, HOW IT
WENT AND WHAT MEMORIES WERE MADE

_____

_____

_____

_____

_____

_____

_____

_____

_____

_____

_____

_____

DAY TWO: YOU'RE SPEAKING MY LANGUAGE

One thing I love about my wife is she is very attentive to detail. When we were dating, she would ask me questions like, *"What is your favorite food? Where is your favorite place to shop? What is your favorite drink at the coffee shop?"* The list goes on. I remember when we were dating, she caught me off guard. She invited me over to her place for dinner for my birthday, and she made my favorite meal in the world, Chicken Piccata. I was blown away that she remembered my favorite dish. She was speaking my language. When I tried a bite, I realized she nailed it, and that she was the one. What made my birthday that day wasn't the gifts, it was the fact that she paid attention to my language. In other words, she was all ears, which meant she valued me. The little things will always take your relationship a long way.

Think of something that speaks your girl's language. Her language could be her favorite drink, favorite food or a favorite candy. Whatever it is, do something that speaks her language. When you do things out of the normal, you will receive abnormal results.

JOURNAL BELOW:

WRITE WHAT YOU LEARNED TODAY, HOW IT WENT AND WHAT MEMORIES WERE MADE

DAY THREE: L.O.L

Rich's Insight:

If there is one thing that I have never heard come out of a woman's mouth is, "*I don't like it when a man makes me laugh.*" In all honesty, laughter is one thing that a woman looks for in a man. Laughter brings joy to your day, it brings a smile to your heart. Therefore we need to laugh more. One thing my wife and I do is we love sending funny memes to each other. There is times when will send non stop memes together on instagram for an hour and will just die in laughter. In those moments of laughter that's when we start to connect to each other and it takes the stress out of our day.

I love what the scripture teaches us in Proverbs 17:22 (NLT), "*A cheerful heart is good medicine, but a crushed spirit dries up the bones.*" Laughter is the cheapest medicine you can take, but it's also the greatest medicine you could give. It will make an indelible difference to your relationship.

Be creative! How can you make your woman laugh today? Send her a meme from Instagram. Watch a comedy together. Maybe it's as simple as reading the jokes on the back of a Laffy Taffy wrapper (let's be honest, those are the best anyway). Or maybe you do some funny dance or antic right after dinner time. Your goal today is to make her laugh!

JOURNAL BELOW:

WRITE WHAT YOU LEARNED TODAY, HOW IT
WENT AND WHAT MEMORIES WERE MADE

DAY FOUR: THE ART OF COMMUNI-CATION

Yesterday Alyssa and I had a little fight. Or disagreement is probably a better word, but you know what I mean. Those times where you're both a little frustrated, and you start getting that feeling in your head. *"I know I'm right. Why doesn't she blank."* You can fill in the blank.

In the disagreement with Alyssa, when I started to think about it, I realized it wasn't because of the reason we were fighting. It was because we didn't properly communicate beforehand. And when you don't communicate, then expectations are not met, and that's usually ground zero for tension, strife and more.

Rich's Insight:
Can we communicate more effectively which one another by listening before we speak? I once heard someone say, *"The reason why God gave you two ears is that he wants you to listen twice as much than you speak."* Let's listen and then speak, rather than listening and then speaking. Let's remind our partner that we are all ears.

Today, ask her how you can communicate better with her. Ask her if there are any instances or things you say or do that frustrate her. Rehash the past few disagreements and ask how you could have communicated better before they happened in order for them to not happen.

JOURNAL BELOW:

WRITE WHAT YOU LEARNED TODAY, HOW IT
WENT AND WHAT MEMORIES WERE MADE

_____

_____

_____

_____

_____

_____

_____

_____

_____

_____

_____

_____

_____

DAY FIVE: WORSHIP

Rich's Insight:

I'll never forget one of my first date nights with my wife, and that's when we went to a Kari Jobe concert. My wife and I were thrilled to see one of our favorite artists. In the moments of worship, I could begin to see God move in our relationship. We glorified God that night, and in return, our hearts were enriched. All this happened because of the power of worship.

When you put on worship, it washes your worries away. When you put on worship, it enriches your spirit and cleanses your mind. There is power in worship. There are moments when we will get into an argument in the car and give each other the silent treatment. We won't say anything to each other, but one of us always ends up putting on some worship music, and sure enough, we find ourselves apologizing to each other because God started to minister to us through worship.

So for today, worship with her. Put on some worship or praise music and watch God begin to move in your hearts. The more you elevate God, the more God will elevate your relationship.

JOURNAL BELOW:

WRITE WHAT YOU LEARNED TODAY, HOW IT
WENT AND WHAT MEMORIES WERE MADE

_____

_____

_____

_____

_____

_____

_____

_____

_____

_____

_____

_____

_____

DAY SIX:
LET IT GO

Just a few hours ago (from the time I am typing this) Alyssa and I got into one of those little disagreements. You know, the disagreement where, by the time you get to the end of it, you can't even remember why you were arguing in the first place.

This one was my fault. I had made a dumb side comment that was meant to be funny, but in retrospect, the comment was just snarky and hurtful. When I made the comment, we were in the grocery store and just about to part ways to conquer and divide our shopping list (the only right way to do it, especially with kids, CAN I GET AN AMEN). It gave me a few minutes to think about it. You know what I realized? It was simply my fault. I was wrong and what I said was hurtful. It was in that moment I felt bad and realized I needed to apologize and ask for forgiveness. A couple of minutes later once we reconvened, I said I was sorry. I asked her to forgive me.

Then it hit me—forgiveness truly is one of the sustaining powers of a relationship. Without it, surely every relationship would venture into realms of resentment, hurt, bitterness, and more. And that stuff can destroy a relationship. I'd say hands down one reason I feel like Alyssa and I have a relatively healthy relationship is we both hold apologies and forgiveness as a non-negotiable. That one will be humble enough to apologize, and one will be graceful enough to accept and speak forgiveness.

Think of one thing you maybe haven't apologized for that you said, did or held onto today, yesterday, or maybe even long ago. And maybe you can't think of anything but talk about forgiveness with your girlfriend and chat about how you can integrate it more into your relationship or do better at it.

JOURNAL BELOW:

WRITE WHAT YOU LEARNED TODAY, HOW IT
WENT AND WHAT MEMORIES WERE MADE

_____

_____

_____

_____

_____

_____

_____

_____

_____

_____

_____

_____

_____

DAY SEVEN: PRESS PLAY

Alyssa and I both came of age or were teenagers at the end of the 90's and beginning of the 2000's. Because of this, we were in the glory days for music playlists. Back then a playlist wasn't just something you made quickly on your iPhone, but it was incredibly thought out and structured. You then burned it onto a CD for your significant other. (Please tell me I'm not the only one remembering this right now.)

Now, I don't want to be the person that is always like, *"Well, back in MY DAY,"* that is classic dad syndrome. But there was something special that has been lost about the making of music mixes we'd gift to each other. I, to this day, still remember a few different ones I made Alyssa while we were dating and even one I made during our break-up that I gave to her after we got back together.

Rich's Insight:
Music not only connects you but when you send a song your lady's way, it lets her know how you feel about her. Shakespeare once said, *"When words fail, music speaks."* If you couldn't say a word and the music would speak for you, what would it say?

Make her a playlist today. Whether it's an iPhone playlist or a CD you burn, speak to her through music. Be thoughtful with the theme-choose either songs that remind you of her, that tell your story, or that represents your relationship.

JOURNAL BELOW:

WRITE WHAT YOU LEARNED TODAY, HOW IT
WENT AND WHAT MEMORIES WERE MADE

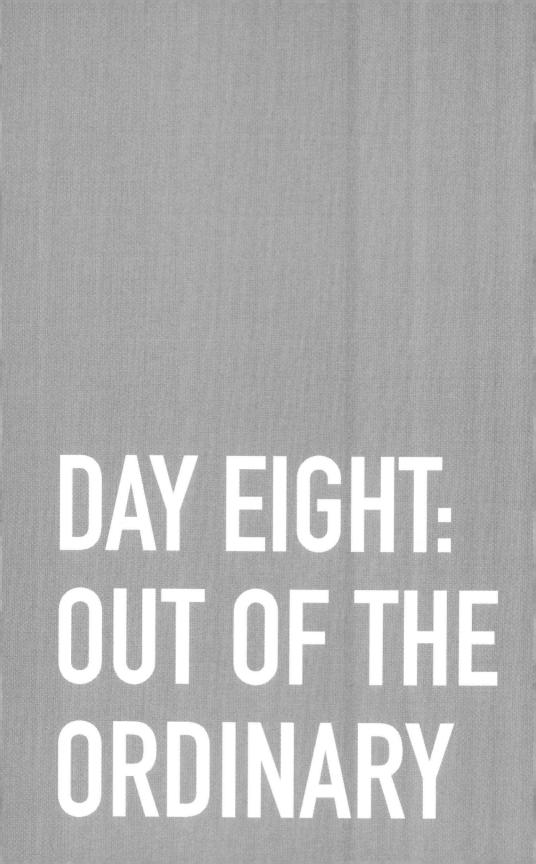

DAY EIGHT: OUT OF THE ORDINARY

Alyssa and I have a pretty good rhythm in the home. You know, who takes out the trash, who does the grocery shopping, and more. For example, I'm the kitchen cleaner upper. Why? Because I'm a little OCD about organization. (I'm that guy that likes vacuuming the carpet because of the lines it makes after you're done.) So that means I do the dishes, wipe down the counters, put the leftover food away, etc. And Alyssa is in charge of grocery shopping and meal planning. Now, of course, neither of these are so rigid we can't each jump in and help each other out once in a while. But normally we do the things we've learned mesh well with our relationship.

Rich's Insight:
We understand the key to a healthy relationship is not to get familiar with each other. Because when familiarity walks in, honor walks out. We grow familiar with each other when we take for granted the things our partner does.

Today or this week, think on one thing that is her *"normal"* responsibility that you can do to surprise her or ask her if you can do something for her. You could offer to do her laundry, get her car washed for her, or clean her house. Take a load off your lady and do something out of the ordinary.

JOURNAL BELOW:

WRITE WHAT YOU LEARNED TODAY, HOW IT
WENT AND WHAT MEMORIES WERE MADE

_____

_____

_____

_____

_____

_____

_____

_____

_____

_____

_____

_____

_____

DAY NINE:
EXPRESS IT

Rich's Insight:

Have you ever had someone say something nice about you? Maybe it was on your birthday, for an accomplishment or just out of the blue for no reason. One thing that I love to do when I preach is to honor my wife. I will usually express how much I love and adore her. I want my wife to know that I am never ashamed of the love I have for her. When I do this, it always melts her heart because I took the time to honor her. Here's what I've realized, an unexpressed compliment isn't a compliment at all.

Instead of making a note in your heart of how much you appreciate her, express it to her today. Think of the top 10 traits or qualities you love about her and express that to her! If you could do this in person, that would be best, but if you won't see her today, then express your love for her on FaceTime. When you express your love for her, it is a gesture she will hold in her heart forever.

JOURNAL BELOW:

WRITE WHAT YOU LEARNED TODAY, HOW IT WENT AND WHAT MEMORIES WERE MADE

_____

_____

_____

_____

DAY TEN: IT'S NOT ABOUT ME

One of the best pieces of advice Alyssa and I ever got about marriage was to always remember that it's about giving, not taking. Or another way to put it is: marriage is about serving, not about getting served.

Think how much that latter one is true, even though we probably wouldn't admit it aloud. We structure our days, say certain things and do certain things in hopes that we would get served or that we would get what we want. Secretly, if our girlfriend or wife doesn't do those things we start to get resentful or contemptuous. We start having that inner dialogue of, *"She should....if only she....I can't believe she expects me to always..."*

One of the biggest joys of life is to get to serve your girlfriend. Service is secretly the key to joy. The reason I say a secret is because most people haven't discovered that. Sure it takes a little bit more time and energy, and sure, sometimes it feels harder than being served. Not many people, once done doing something for someone, think, *"Wow! Well, that was a total waste."* No. We realize it did something for us. It created joy, not only for us but the person we served.

Rich's Insight:
Serving creates selflessness in you and destroys being selfish. That's what relationships are about being selfless. The moment you are about me, myself and I, the relationship will slowly die. The moment you turn your eyes off of *"me"* and place them on *"we"* is when the relationship will thrive. We have to remind ourselves that it's not about me, it's about us.

I encourage you to do one act of service today for your girlfriend. Ask her how you can serve her today and however that may be, do it cheerfully.

JOURNAL BELOW:

WRITE WHAT YOU LEARNED TODAY, HOW IT
WENT AND WHAT MEMORIES WERE MADE

_____

_____

_____

_____

_____

_____

_____

_____

_____

_____

_____

_____

DAY ELEVEN: DATE NIGHT WITH THE WISE

Rich's Insight:

I found the greatest way to grow your relationship is to learn from other couples. From couples who are prospering in their relationship and who conquered mountains that you're trying to conquer. The Bible teaches us in Proverbs 16:16 (NIV), *"How much better to get wisdom than gold."* The key to a prosperous relationship is to reap wisdom from a prosperous relationship.

My wife and I will go out with other couples and will ask them questions. Questions like, *"What strengthens a marriage?"* *"If there's one thing that will keep a relationship in unity what would it be?"* The list goes on. What are we doing? We are reaping wisdom from other couples.

This week, take a couple you look up to out for a date night or invite them over. Ask them questions that will improve your relationship. Most of all have fun and learn from them.

JOURNAL BELOW:

WRITE WHAT YOU LEARNED TODAY, HOW IT WENT AND WHAT MEMORIES WERE MADE

_____

_____

_____

DAY TWELVE: ACROSS THE TABLE

I love food. Like, seriously, love food. For example, I have a minor obsession with Chipotle...that guac though! Food is something that really ties together mine and Alyssa's relationship. We both believe in eating good food, having good meals, while enjoying good conversation. Food is almost the scrapbook for all our adventures the past four years. We remember most adventures and trips by where we ate and what restaurant was the best.

If you are like most everyone else, you eat around three meals per day. Breakfast, lunch, and dinner. Sadly one of the things we've lost in our culture is to make food more about efficiency or worship. We either worship the food (i.e., we are tempted to have a poor relationship with food by not stewarding it well and taking care of our bodies) or we see it as nutrients only (we calorie count, we do the math, etc.). Food is neither. It's an incredibly beautiful gift from our Creator that has the beautiful blessing of being a natural relationship builder. It's why most of us feel slightly weird eating alone. I'll be honest though, I'm pretty introverted and like a solo meal, just like I like going to the movies alone too, but I digress. Food is an opportunity to sit at the table, look eye to eye and build relationships. You laugh, cry, love and grow at the table. And not to mention how much fun it is to cook before the food even gets to the table.

Use food to your advantage today. Use food in a way that builds your relationship. That could mean cooking a meal for her. That could mean taking her out to her favorite restaurant. It could mean both of you purposely trying something unique you have never tried, just to have fun. Whatever it is, use food for what it is today-an easy opportunity get to grow closer to the person across the table.

JOURNAL BELOW:

WRITE WHAT YOU LEARNED TODAY, HOW IT
WENT AND WHAT MEMORIES WERE MADE

_____

_____

_____

_____

_____

_____

_____

_____

_____

_____

_____

_____

_____

DAY THIRTEEN: HER WORLD

I absolutely love *Back To The Future*. It's my favorite movie of all time. In my office I have a *Back To The Future* poster, Marty and Doc figurines, as well a now discontinued Deloran Lego set. To say I'm a fan is an understatement. In fact, I always know other fans based on my constant use of one-liners from the film. *("There's that word again, heavy. Is there something wrong with the earth's gravitational pull in the future?")* I know they aren't a fan if I drop a line and they just stare blankly.

When I got married, I wanted to see if my wife was a BTTF fan too but to my surprise, she hadn't seen the movie yet. We ended up watching it on our honeymoon. I remember watching it with Alyssa and being able to tell she thought it was a fun and good movie, but didn't think it was life-changing like I did. If my memory serves me correctly, we've even watched it since then. Alyssa isn't a huge fan but keeps watching it. Why? She wants to enter into my world. She wants to know the one-liners so she can use them with me. She wants to watch the movie because she wants to get just that much closer to me.

Entering into the world of your girlfriend is vital to a healthy relationship. It gives you the wisdom and insight to help and lift your partner up. So when they're having a tough day, you know how to cheer your partner up. Or you know the right words or right things to do to keep your relationship vibrant and healthy. It always saddens me when I see a couple, and it's very much a *"he does his thing, she does her thing"* type of relationship. Good and fun relationships enter into each other's spaces. How can you enter her world today?

Maybe that means there is something she likes you can research a bit before dinner, so you can have a fun conversation with her about it while you eat. Or maybe it means you can you get a pedicure with her. This one isn't all that bad even though us guys hate it. Someone who is cleaning my feet, making them look good and then ending it all with a foot massage-fine by me!

JOURNAL BELOW:

WRITE WHAT YOU LEARNED TODAY, HOW IT
WENT AND WHAT MEMORIES WERE MADE

DAY FOURTEEN: DREAM CHASERS

Alyssa and I were only dating at the time, but I remember when she started to mention how she was looking to find a new hobby. Photography was something she mentioned as one of those possible hobbies. So I filed that away and waited. Waited to see if any of those listed bubbled back up. And again photography did. She mentioned how she wanted to start getting into it but didn't have a camera. The problem is I was broke and couldn't buy her a camera. She had a good steady job though and soon enough, bought a camera. A few months went by, and she started to get really into it but didn't have that good of a lens.

I started saving. I had some photography friends I'd text and message asking them what good lenses were. Finally I bought a lens and surprised her with it. What's awesome is she's been able to take pictures of families, high schoolers and more with that camera.

See, in a relationship both of the people will have dreams, hopes, and plans. Either a skill they wish they had or something they've been saving up for awhile and the list goes on and on. Maybe she wants to get better at cooking. Maybe she wants to learn the piano. If you can think back on recurring themes on the past few months or years of your relationship-what would one be that she wants to do but hasn't gone for it yet?

Today's challenge is to encourage your girlfriend by re-opening the conversation about plans she put on the back burner. This could mean buying her a cookbook or finding free YouTube videos on cooking. Then maybe write out a card or note about how much you love to see her chase her passions and dreams and how you're her biggest cheerleader.

JOURNAL BELOW:

WRITE WHAT YOU LEARNED TODAY, HOW IT
WENT AND WHAT MEMORIES WERE MADE

_____

_____

_____

_____

_____

_____

_____

_____

_____

_____

_____

_____

DAY FIFTEEN: THE POWER OF YOUR BEEN THROUGH

Stories are powerful. Whether we realize it or not, we think in story. We are not mindless computers absorbing data. We give that data flesh. The data gets humanized. It gets storied. And a lot of times, a story is the very way we remember our past and look towards the future. As a couple, we know this is true. We don't see our relationships as random abstract things but instead the crazy story of how two lives intersected and never were the same again.

I mean, if you've been together for any length of time, you know when asked about your love story, it's something you almost begin to memorize. The cookie cutter version. I realized the other day, that every time I tell the story of Alyssa and I, I feel this little spark of joy and gratitude that I ended up with her. There's something about recounting your story that gives your relationship strength. The good, the bad, the easy, the hard, the breakup, the kids, the first date or that awkward first kiss. (Which Alyssa and I definitely had. That's a story for another time though.)

One of the biggest joys of life is to get to serve your wife or girlfriend. Service is actually secretly the key to joy. The reason I say secret is because most people haven't discovered that. Sure it takes a little bit more time and energy and sure, sometimes it feels harder than being served. Not many people, once done doing something for someone, thinks, *"Wow! Well that was a total waste."* No. We realize it did something in us. It created joy, not only in us, but the person we served.

Rich's Insight:

Reminds you of how faithful God is, and it gives you the motivation to keep moving forward. There's power in your been through because what you've been through it sets you up for your future break through.

Today, spend time talking about your love story. Talk about the hard times so far. And then talk about the good times. Then, the most fun part, I think, is talk about when you do this again in, say, ten years, what do you want your story to be? What do the next ten years look like for your relationship?

JOURNAL BELOW:

WRITE WHAT YOU LEARNED TODAY, HOW IT WENT AND WHAT MEMORIES WERE MADE

DAY SIXTEEN: I'M ALL EARS

By nature, I'm a fixer. I like to tinker with things, take them apart, put them back together. When something doesn't go the way I planned, I start analyzing it and wondering how I can fix it. My fixer tendency is a good trait most of the time. But if I'm not careful, this can be hurtful to Alyssa.

Whenever she is feeling down, something bad happened, or she just needs to talk, the last thing she wants me to do is to try and fix it. In fact, she'll even say in some of our discussions, *"Don't try to fix it, just listen."* When you listen to her you're saying, *"I'm all ears,"* and since you are all ears, what you're communicating to her is that your heart is fully invested in her. Now, of course, I'm just trying to be helpful when I try to solve the problem, but I'm trying to be helpful on my terms, not hers.

Rich's Insight:

To truly love someone, you love them on their terms. Meaning you offer encouragement, blessing, love, kind words, etc. in a way that they best receive, not the way you best receive. For Alyssa and most (but not all) girls, listening is huge. Often listening is the greatest encouragement you could give them. They want to feel listened to. Heard. Seen. (Shoot, this isn't just a girl thing because I guess I'm that way too. It's natural to desire to feel understood.)

So how can you listen better today? Make a special point to not talk as fast. Ask double the amount of questions you usually do. Or say, *"Can you tell me more about that?"* or *"Why do you like that or feel that way, etc.?"*

JOURNAL BELOW:

WRITE WHAT YOU LEARNED TODAY, HOW IT
WENT AND WHAT MEMORIES WERE MADE

_____

_____

_____

_____

_____

_____

_____

_____

_____

_____

_____

_____

DAY SEVENTEEN: IT'S NOT YOUR JOB

"Consider how tough it is to change yourself and you'll understand what little chance you have in trying to change others." -Jacob M. Braude

If that above quote isn't a smack in the face, I don't know what is. In a relationship, once the butterflies and such start wearing off, you start to notice things. Things start to annoy you, bother you, frustrate you and upset you about the other person (and they certainly start to notice those things about you). One of the temptations is to want to change the person. You think *if only they would change this one thing, life would be a lot easier or better.* And while that might be the case, you'll realize your efforts are probably futile.

Trying to change the other person for your benefit in a relationship only brings more hurt, pain, and heartache. Now don't get me wrong, change is good, and both of you will change over time, but Alyssa and I have both noticed that's best done through prayer, encouragement, and the Holy Spirit. Instead of Alyssa or I telling each other about something we think needs to change, we start praying for that person and ask God to either A) show them the area they need to change or B) show ourselves where maybe we have an area for growth. It might be harder, but better, than trying to change them.

Rich's Insight:
Remember, we are called to inspire our partner not change our partner. God does the changing; we do the encouraging. If God isn't changing the situation right away, it's probably because He wants to change something in you first.

Think on one thing that you want to change about your girlfriend. Now really dig deep and ask in what ways could you change on that issue? For example, I hate making the bed and Alyssa loves to make the bed. We fought about it off and on for a year in our marriage. I tried so hard to change her. And finally, God convicted me and said if she wanted it made, then I should serve and love her in that way. So now it gets made every morning, and I haven't brought it up since. What can you change about yourself today?

JOURNAL BELOW:

WRITE WHAT YOU LEARNED TODAY, HOW IT WENT AND WHAT MEMORIES WERE MADE

_____

_____

_____

_____

_____

_____

_____

DAY EIGHTEEN: COMPLIMENTS BRING CONFIDENCE

Words are an interesting thing. They have immense power. Compliments are one of those things. I've noticed lately though that compliments have different levels of power based on who is giving it. A stranger might compliment me and I'm encouraged but when Alyssa compliments me it does so much more. Why? Because I'm closest to Alyssa and she's the love of my life. When the person who loves you and knows you still compliments you, that has power.

Rich's Insight:
Compliments bring confidence, and if they bring confidence, then we should do more of it. We should encourage our partner on a daily basis. No other person besides God should take the role of being our partners greatest cheerleader. Encouragement always brings nourishment to our relationship.

So, not only give intentional compliments to your fiance or girlfriend today but go one step further. Every time you compliment her, write it down on your phone or a piece of paper. Then at the end of the day, give her the paper or a note with all of the compliments on it to show her how much you care about her and spoke life to her today.

JOURNAL BELOW:

WRITE WHAT YOU LEARNED TODAY, HOW IT WENT AND WHAT MEMORIES WERE MADE

DAY NINETEEN: WE'RE GOING TO GET THROUGH THIS

Harriet Ann Jacobs was famous for saying, *"There are no bonds so strong as those which are formed by suffering together."* If someone were to ask me what things Alyssa and I have gone through in marriage that made us grow the most or strengthened our marriage-it'd no doubt be the hard things. Relationships, financial things, the tough news we got from a friend, etc. Every time it's hard walking through it but looking back there is something special about hardships that act as glue when walked through together.

Of course, that doesn't mean we should be going hunting for hardships. It also doesn't mean we should avoid them. So many times in relationships we try to do everything in our power to take the easiest road, make the easiest decision or do whatever will cause the least amount of tension or toughness. What you have to understand is growth isn't found by what's easy, it is found by what's most challenging. Hard times create strong relationships. Long roads create a deep appreciation for life.

Rich's Insight:
What if instead of dreading those moments, we embraced them? What if we didn't search them out, but when they landed on our doorstep, we welcomed them as moments to grow together in a way that prosperity or success never could?

Today, reflect on a hardship you and your girlfriend have gone through in your relationship. Talk about how it grew you together and what you learned from it.

JOURNAL BELOW:

WRITE WHAT YOU LEARNED TODAY, HOW IT
WENT AND WHAT MEMORIES WERE MADE

_____

_____

_____

_____

_____

_____

_____

_____

_____

_____

_____

_____

_____

DAY TWENTY: WASH FEET

I still remember the day I proposed to Alyssa. I had my two friends go before us to this secluded beach where they'd set the scene before we got there. They put out rose petals, lit candles and hung up pictures from our relationship lining the pathway down from the car to the beach.

And when I got down to the bottom, there was a blanket and a bottle of champagne. It's hard for me to remember every little detail because it was such a blur (and I was so nervous). One thing I do remember is that before I proposed, I got down on my knees, took out a thermos of warm water and a washcloth from my backpack and began to wash her feet. I then proceeded to tell her I wanted this to be a symbol of our relationship, of me serving her and lifting her up in every regard...and then I asked her to marry me.

There's something about foot washing that is incredibly humbling. It feels a little awkward, yet holy. It's been a picture for thousands of years of service, originating in antiquity where foot washing was more of a necessity in many desert climates. While feet washing might not be as needed, it's still just as powerful of a picture to show care and affection.

Rich's Insight:
Service is what relationships should be about, serving one another. We should stay in a state of humility by serving one another. Washing feet is not only a great reminder of serving each other, but it's also a reminder that we are going to walk this out together. That even when life gets dirty, and the road is tough that we will walk it out and conquer life together.

Wash her feet today. Remind her of how much you honor and respect her. Ultimately though, let her know how much you care and how you enjoy serving her.

JOURNAL BELOW:

WRITE WHAT YOU LEARNED TODAY, HOW IT
WENT AND WHAT MEMORIES WERE MADE

_____

_____

_____

_____

_____

_____

_____

_____

_____

_____

_____

_____

DAY TWENTY-ONE: THINK OUTSIDE OF THE BOX

I was in love with making forts as a kid. I'd get all the sheets, pillows, chairs and anything else I could use around the house to build these intricate forts right in the middle of the living room. My mom wasn't always a huge fan (for the simple fact the whole house looked a tornado went through it), but she let me do it nonetheless.

There's something about making a fort that creates this fun sense of adventure and imagination. In fact, that's one thing I think we sorely lack these days, especially in romantic relationships. Imagination is no longer a thing celebrated for your whole life. Creativity is no longer a muscle we routinely work out. Both of these things are seen as traits to be left in childhood.

What if I told you creativity, adventure and imagination is sometimes the key to a fun and healthy relationship? Thinking outside of the box, mixing it up every once in awhile and doing things you wouldn't normally do helps jumpstart a relationship.

Rich's Insight:
When we lose creativity, we invite familiarity into our relationship. Our relationships should be full of life; it should be full of awe and wonder. If our relationships are boring and stagnant, it stems from us not being creative and stirring things up.

Today be creative. Do something you normally wouldn't do. Go and paint with each other, write poetry together, take a cooking class, Or shoot photos of each other. Whatever you do, get out of the box.

JOURNAL BELOW:

WRITE WHAT YOU LEARNED TODAY, HOW IT
WENT AND WHAT MEMORIES WERE MADE

_____

_____

_____

_____

_____

_____

_____

_____

_____

_____

_____

_____

_____

DAY TWENTY-TWO: TAKE A WALK

One of Alyssa's favorite things is to go for a walk. She usually goes every day, whether to just get out or get a good workout. To her, if she doesn't go for a walk, she feels a little pent up or closed in being inside all day. I am not a huge fan of walks. I am more so now than before, but for awhile I pretty much hated them. I didn't like doing any physical activity that wasn't also fun at the same time (basketball, swimming, etc.). I've started to change a little and now go with Alyssa on a lot of those walks. You know what's funny? There's something about walks that just renew your energy and spirit for the day. Also, the conversations are always good.

Rich's Insight:

When we go on our walks, we find ourselves dreaming about the future, and we reflect on all that God has done in our lives. In those moments we get away from the busyness of life, and we begin to tune into our own lives. There have been times on our walks where God would place a burden on our hearts to pray about certain things. So we would walk and start praying. When we finished our walks and got back into our car, it's as if God brought new life into us.

Today, go for a walk. Could be around the neighborhood or you could drive somewhere and then walk. Doesn't have to be big. Just walk, chat, hangout and relax.

JOURNAL BELOW:

WRITE WHAT YOU LEARNED TODAY, HOW IT
WENT AND WHAT MEMORIES WERE MADE

_____

_____

_____

_____

_____

_____

_____

_____

_____

_____

_____

_____

_____

DAY TWENTY-THREE: BRING IT BACK

When you first start dating, you're on your best behavior. You do things and say things to impress but also shower kindness on her. For example, it's common gentlemen etiquette to open the door for her, pull out her chair, bring flowers and more.

For some reason, if you've been dating for any length of time, this stuff starts to fade and no longer happens. But shouldn't it be the opposite? If the love and connection are growing, shouldn't that stuff at least stay the same or grow as well?

Rich's Insight:
The challenge is never to allow your relationship to grow comfortable. It grows comfortable when we become complacent. I've realized that sometimes if I want my relationship to get ahead, I need to look back. Looking back reminds you of what the little things you once did to catch your lady's attention. Don't allow the fire to grow dim in your relationship because you are too lazy to place another wood in the fire. Fires last when the supply of wood is present. Be present with her and keep showering her with love.

Today, ask yourself what you can bring back that you did when you first began dating. What small gesture can you continually do as an encouragement to her? Maybe that means open the door for her again, bring her flowers or compliment her.

JOURNAL BELOW:

WRITE WHAT YOU LEARNED TODAY, HOW IT
WENT AND WHAT MEMORIES WERE MADE

_____

_____

_____

_____

_____

_____

_____

_____

_____

_____

_____

_____

_____

DAY TWENTY-FOUR: CHEESY PICK UP-LINES

I'm a big fan of cheesiness. I'm the king of bad jokes, and I love the ridiculous pick-up lines. Just ask Alyssa. At this point, she just barely laughs and makes a face that somewhat communicates, *"Man, I sure got lucky marrying this guy."*

My favorite thing to do is to surprise her with pick-up lines or bad jokes all throughout the day, especially when she least expects it. We haven't even gotten out of bed, and I'll say, *"Do you have a band-aid? Because I scraped my knee falling for you."*

There's something about them that just brings a joy and spontaneity to our relationship that is fun. It makes her laugh and when you can make your fiance or girlfriend laugh, you know there's nothing better.

The task for today is to hop on Google and find ten of your favorite cheesy pick-up lines. Then spread them out throughout the day. You can call her or text them to her. Watch out! She will probably fall in love with you all over again!

JOURNAL BELOW:
WRITE WHAT YOU LEARNED TODAY, HOW IT WENT AND WHAT MEMORIES WERE MADE

_____

_____

_____

_____

DAY TWENTY-FIVE: ATTITUDE OF GRATITUDE

I once heard a quote that said, *"It's not happy people who are thankful, it's thankful people who are happy."* I couldn't agree more. Most don't realize that thankfulness is the secret to joy. The reason I call it a secret is it seems many haven't caught on yet! In the Bible, thankfulness is elevated almost to the place of being the heart of worship. A thankful heart is what God is looking for and pleased in. When we are thankful, it brings Him glory, and it brings us joy. In fact, the Bible even says that thankfulness is the will of God! (1 Thessalonians 5:18). A lot of times we think the will of God is this mystical thing like what joy we are to take or what passion we should pursue- when the Bible says just being thankful is His will.

Rich's Insight:

When we create an attitude of gratitude, it changes the dynamic of our relationship. It reminds us of how blessed we are and how faithful God has been. We need to be intentional when it comes to thankfulness because it is so easy to complain about what we don't have. The passage (1 Thessalonians 5:18) reminds us to be thankful in all circumstances. Do you know why? Because every circumstance we're in is a set up for God to do something amazing in our life.

That's the task for today. Be Thankful. If you have an iPhone or a little sketch pad, go on the hunt for things you are thankful for in her and about her throughout the day and write every them down. Feel free to write down even the littlest things. By the end of the day, you should have dozens of reasons, if not hundreds! Dwell on the list that night or maybe even show her all the reasons you are thankful for her.

JOURNAL BELOW:

WRITE WHAT YOU LEARNED TODAY, HOW IT
WENT AND WHAT MEMORIES WERE MADE

_____

_____

_____

_____

_____

_____

_____

_____

_____

_____

_____

_____

_____

DAY TWENTY-SIX: LOVE LETTER

There's something about a handwritten note that just seems a little more thoughtful and memorable sometimes. You could say the same thing in a letter that you could in a text, and it'd feel more tangible and worth saving.

In fact, Alyssa to this day still has all the letters I wrote to her over the years. Some dating back 7 or so years. I even used to spray my cologne on some of the letters when we were dating long distance so when she opened the envelope, it'd smell a little like me. I know, I know, my game was on point at that stage in my life. Thank goodness we didn't start dating in middle school or else those letters would smell like Axe body spray (AKA middle school boys locker room forever). Letters have a way of even making you, the writer, think things through or say things a little differently.

Rich's Insight:
Letters hold history. There are times when I have randomly opened a letter from the past, and as I read it, the letter gave me hope and inspiration. It brought back memories and reminded me of all that we've been through and how we felt at that particular time. Letters have a way of bringing you back to the past and bringing you encouragement for your future.

A letter received in the mail is the most exciting. Today, write your girl a love letter and mail it to her. Don't tell her what your encouragement challenge is today. Instead, let her be surprised when she receives it in her mailbox in a couple of days.

JOURNAL BELOW:

WRITE WHAT YOU LEARNED TODAY, HOW IT
WENT AND WHAT MEMORIES WERE MADE

_____

_____

_____

_____

_____

_____

_____

_____

_____

_____

_____

_____

DAY TWENTY–SEVEN: WEEKLY JOURNAL

One of my favorite things Alyssa and I do every week is we get away for about an hour and go through what we call our *"marriage journal."* Alyssa's parents watch the kiddos, and we head off to the beach or somewhere restful and go through the journal. It's a journal we keep that has 5-7 questions we ask ourselves every week and then record the answers in there. It's changed the whole dynamic of our relationship in regards to us communicating well, squashing certain things before they turn big and understand more about each other. Also, it's fun to have a written record of your relationship and how you are doing in different seasons.

We got the idea and questions from a friend and had loved doing it ever since. The cool part is you have full control over it to make it different or the same. The questions we ask are:

1) What brought you joy this week?
2) What's something that was hard this week?
3) What's one specific thing I can do for you this week?
4) How can I pray for you this week?
5) Is there anything that's gone unsaid this week?
6) What's a dream or thought that's been on the forefront of your mind this week?

And then once a month we ask ourselves how we are doing. In all honesty, it's been life-changing for us to do this journal. I get to hear how Alyssa's week has been hard when maybe before I wasn't paying attention all that well. Also, I get to hear how I can serve her in the week ahead. Journaling gives you insights to create a better relationship.

Rich's Insight:
Emma Watson once said, *"Journaling allows me to get things out of my head and work them out in a way that feels safe."* When we journal privately, it helps us to work things out publicly. Because journaling allows us to be transparent and when we are transparent with each other we can help each other.

Today find some journal around the house or get a brand new one. Game plan how you and she are going to do your relationship journal and either keep or edit the questions we ask. Commit to getting away or spending one hour together on it every week.

JOURNAL BELOW:

WRITE WHAT YOU LEARNED TODAY, HOW IT WENT AND WHAT MEMORIES WERE MADE

_____

_____

_____

_____

_____

_____

_____

_____

_____

_____

_____

DAY TWENTY-EIGHT: GOOD MORNING TEXT

Rich's Insight:

When I wake up in the morning one of the first things, I'll do besides seeking the Lord is seeking my cell phone. As I go through my cell phone, I get a list of notifications. Usually texts, social media notifications, and email messages. I tend to find myself looking at the text messages first because I want to know what people are inquiring of me. The text I love to receive the most are the ones with encouragement because they bring fresh fire for my day.

When my wife and I started dating, that's what I did. I would send her texts of encouragement so when she woke up she had something encouraging to read to start her day. Proverbs 16:24 (NLT) teaches us that *"Kind words are like honey, sweet to the soul and healthy for the body."* Healthy couples know how to send encouraging words.

This challenge requires you to set your alarm early so you can write her a sweet, good morning text. Tell her how much you honor, love and appreciate her. Your text will drastically change her day.

JOURNAL BELOW:

WRITE WHAT YOU LEARNED TODAY, HOW IT WENT AND WHAT MEMORIES WERE MADE

_____

_____

_____

_____

DAY TWENTY-NINE: STAND ON THIS SCRIPTURE

The Scriptures are such a powerful thing. They are active, living and God's very own word. They can breathe life into a relationship when that relationship comes under the beauty of it.

For Alyssa and I, scripture is everything. Both of us try to read at least a few minutes each day (even though with two young kids that is a tough task). It anchors our relationship and reminds us of what's important, and what matters. Ultimately the better I follow Jesus, the better I can serve my wife. And the more I drift from Jesus, the more I realize I'm not loving and serving my wife well. A relationship that prioritizes the scriptures as a center point for them and their relationship is one that will flourish.

Rich's Insight:
What we've realized is if we aren't spiritually fed we will be emotionally led. When you're full of the word, you will be led by the word, but when you're full of yourself, you will make a fool out of yourself. Let's be spiritually led by getting fed with the scriptures. A couple is only as strong as what they stand for. So let's stand on the word and see our lives flourish.

Today find a scripture passage that you want to dwell on for the next month in regards to your relationship. It can be a verse you want to remind yourself of to serve her better, or it can be one you both agree on as your *"relationship verse"* for the next month.

JOURNAL BELOW:

WRITE WHAT YOU LEARNED TODAY, HOW IT
WENT AND WHAT MEMORIES WERE MADE

_____

_____

_____

_____

_____

_____

_____

_____

_____

_____

_____

_____

_____

DAY THIRTY: CLEANING UP THE PAST

You can tell a lot by a looking inside a person's car. If you looked inside of mine you'd realize I have two kids (two car seats), I'm not that clean, and I like a good clean air freshener. The car to a lot of people is a second home or space since they use it every day to get around, get to work, run errands and more.

I still remember to this day both mine and Alyssa's cars when we were dating. Oh, how many memories those cars hold. Us going on our first dates, late night drives to get food, and of course our epic listening sessions of old Disney songs or N'Sync throwbacks where I blew a speaker.

Rich's Insight:
Cars hold memories, but cars also hold history. Meaning in her car there could be trash, old items that need to be thrown away, or washing that needs to be done. What greater way to drive forward in the future with a nice cleaning of the past.

Today the challenge is to do something with her car that serves her. That could mean washing her car. It could mean vacuuming the inside of the car. Or it could mean simply leaving little notes all around her car (the dashboard, the glovebox, under the seat, in the trunk). Pick one and have fun!

JOURNAL BELOW:

WRITE WHAT YOU LEARNED TODAY, HOW IT
WENT AND WHAT MEMORIES WERE MADE

_____

_____

_____

_____

_____

_____

_____

_____

_____

_____

_____

_____

_____

_____

DAY THIRTY-ONE: DREAM BOARD

Rich's Insight:

C.S Lewis once said, *"You are never too old to set another goal or to dream a new dream."* I believe dreams are the heartbeat of any relationship and once you lose your dream, you lose the beat of your relationship. Your dream is what gives your relationship drive. It gives you fire for your day and reminds you of what you're working to accomplish together. Dreams matter because dreams are consistently creating a new future.

The Bible teaches us that, *"Where there is no vision, the people perish."* Proverbs 29:18 KJV. In other words, when we don't have a vision, we walk around aimlessly. My wife and I make sure we have a vision we can run with so we create a dream board. A dream board is when you get a small canvas, and you cut out pictures from old magazines that are in alignment with your dreams. Once you cut the photos glue them onto your canvas; and now you have a dream board. When the dream board is done, hang it in your room or office to remind yourself of what you're fighting for.

That's the assignment for today. Create a dream board. Have fun with your girlfriend as the two of you create your dream boards. I encourage you to look at your dream board to remind yourself of what you're fighting for. We would love to see your dream boards as well so make sure you hashtag #31creativeways.

JOURNAL BELOW:

WRITE WHAT YOU LEARNED TODAY, HOW IT
WENT AND WHAT MEMORIES WERE MADE

_____

_____

_____

_____

_____

_____

_____

_____

_____

_____

_____

_____

DAY THIRTY-TWO: YOUR TURN

You didn't think there was going to be a day 32, did ya? We thought we'd add one more day, to turn it over to you. Think of any idea, any gesture, or any kind thing you can do for your significant other today. Be creative. Be loving. And most of all show them how much you care. Also, we'd love to hear what you picked for day 32! We might even end up including it in future versions or volumes of this book. You can upload your idea at *upload.31creativeways.com*. We can't wait to hear how creative you guys are and what y'all came up with!

JOURNAL BELOW:
WRITE DOWN ANY IDEA, GESTURE OR KIND THING YOU CAN DO FOR YOUR SIGNIFICANT OTHER

A NOTE FROM US AFTER FINISHING THIS BOOK

First off, you all rock! For reals. Complete rockstars. Why? You are putting effort into and care about your relationship. You're investing in it. You believe in it. It matters to you.

We believe that a relationship is like a garden. For it to flourish, it needs proper nourishment, constant care, awareness of the things trying to hurt it, and sometimes is a little messy. This book is just a start to hopefully continuing or taking that leap of putting you and your significant other on the path to a vibrant and beautiful relationship.

So thank you for doing this journey with us. Thank you for reading this book. And thank you for just being you. We'd love to hear from you and how the challenge went by sharing something online with the hashtag #31creativeways. We are constantly on that hashtag to see all the awesome stuff you guys are doing, ways you tweaked one of our challenges to make it better and to see all the fun you're having!

For those who maybe are getting this as a gift or don't know much about us, below are just a few other things we have created and done over the past few years. **We hope they encourage you!**

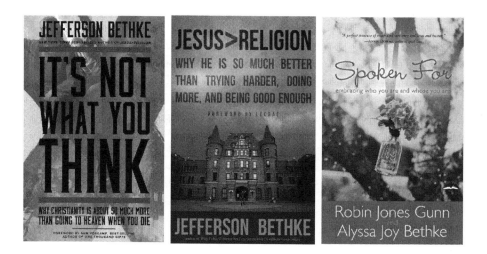

Find at
JEFFBETHKE.COM

Find at
BETHKEWORKSHOPS.COM

WHERE
TO FIND
US
ONLINE